HOLY GHOST MESSAGES

Editor, Kathy Tyrity, BSBA

Vol. 1, No. 1

A magazine on how to give messages from the Holy Ghost, the Angels, or God Power in church.

Including the Epistle for the Holy Alliance Church based on messages, LOVE, and healing. A church of love.

Also including scriptures from Mark and others.

All Rights Reserved
Forest Gnomes Publishing Co.

BALTIC MYSTIC SEA ENTERTAINMENT, Inc.

Hello friends and readers. I am a channel with the God Energy and the Holy Spirit.

I am purely Christian and have been ordained as a reverend. Please accept these newsletters which will eventually become a magazine as my contribution to the sorry state that the world is in and my hope for peace and prosperity.

I will be giving you channeled material which God ordains, and I believe the prophecy that has been given me. It is a gentle spirit that God lends to let you know there are better times ahead. I do believe that. But we have to hang on through several more years of difficult examination.

We are self-examining in these intrepid times. Here are the words that have been given to me through the Holy Ghost that I ask for each day. Some are in the form of short stories and essays. Send them to whom you please and you may write with your comments. If you have questions, send them sincerely stated and we will try to get the answers. Thank you for your readership and your concern about the world.

PROPHECY

Get out of bed at 7 and we will take it from there.

Destruction may be due if the shift of the axis occurs severely. I think much of that is better now. But the shift may affect parts of Florida, Central America, the West, and New York. Central U.S. may have famine but much has been done to correct that. The west half of Asia may have fighting or fire, or something I'm not sure.

We will shore up the possible destruction with world harmony. All of the U.S. may be chaotic during the Middle East wars. There will be war and peace. The cue for this girl is to be watchful and help our cities across the U.S. We can give you details.

And now . . .

Epistle for the Holy Alliance Church

In the 700 great people who fought for the world for centuries love. God of Love. Lord is good. We have several lordships in Holy Alliance. Kent, Sheila, etc. Sheila is like a god of practical living and very necessary to make home a happy place. Becky and Donna are godships of love. And Kathy is a healing energy and god power. And Johnny Fat Jackson is Happiness god and love. If someone reminds you of happiness or love he is someone to go to for this and answers you need in your life. He or she can do stuff for you. We had thought that pictures of those like Kathy and some who died for the world would be circulated to help heal and protect. Look at their eyes to heal.

Linda and Kathy are sisters and somewhat mixed in Kathy; precious to God. We are in several states now. And the Lord's people are still some of us. If possible we will have a church someday and helps there. If you need a healing call either a K or someone who loves you very much.

Almost all hands heal and the Lord heals those who love him. Love will be our main goal from now on with these people. There is a portion of the biblical/prophetic/new life material missing, and it will be typed up soon.

Jesus the First said one way to get love is to fight for something and get it and then you feel really love. I think passion spurs up love and we need to develop this by dreaming over and over our love. Both ideas are very good. See Love Book ("Hey There Lonely Love") or "Brilliant Day."

The 700 people should feel very good because the U.S. is great large and South America was lit up in the picture, too.

The second Lord that the people knew will take charge of maintenance and love. The second Jesus was necessary for love some thought because Jesus Number One hadn't finished the Plan. Jesus number one will still be a healer and love; and his Lord will allow prayer to people who love him and whom He loves.

(pause)

Looking your best is truly essential if you want love. One of us works with styles and colors for hair, dress, make-up and self assurance for all the people he sees who may need this help. He is godlike of Beauty and likes the best for Earth.

(pause)

In 1986 a woman who is now a power of the universe and has the love of nearly every broken-hearted person and god alike did experience Jesus death for the love of the New Era on earth and duty. She loved the undone child of Katie who couldn't hear or see the parade. "I was having touble with my marriage and I was loving Katie so much because I was seeing her so much in so many difficult situations. I saw Katie leaving the world out of her pants, her Spirit coming completely out in a hospital and thought I could usher in the New Age for her. I blew my head off. The evil in the world put Kathy in a situation she could not hope to understand because her divinity and all such things had been stripped by Evil. There should be no evil in the New Era." She, Mrs. Sheila in spirit, was a most beautiful exquisite woman who had understanding of good and the world. Her love is worth hoping for. Kathy has a nothing and no real love left. There would not be a love for a new saving grace like that. She did get a gift though, and has written her heart out to leave behind. Mrs. Sheila's essence was spelled up in a sister whom Kathy loves more than anyone. Kathy can't believe Mrs. Sheila was watching every moment there was such injustice. There will never be justice to that great a degree for Kathy. She hopes for peace. Kathy dearly prays for the New Age of Earth so that all will read the new biblical type material she has, etc. and love itself. Kathy knows. But she has been dwindled to a very mixed up love with nothing to do except take two hours to make lunch or clean up blood. Mrs. Sheila in spirit was not even a relative but someone's classmate who knew Kathy. Sheila was the true love of the world. And she wanted to be. Kathy never knew what she wanted to be because she had to be told by a psychic and then do it and get hell from churches for going to mediums. Some of the psychics she went to spelled her a bag of mistake, too.

AND NOW . . .

From the Broken Hearted people

We love the sister. We like her. We left our wives. We love Kathy. We want God of Love. We have nothing. We do go to church. God of Love not there. We slightly evil. We enjoy love with caring individuals. Kathy's sister says stay with us. Lord tells us about our lives. Kathy is a Love. But sometimes we're undone. Believe. We like ourselves. We are holy.

Earth's reply: "I'm for the Holy.":

(pause ...)

Jesus and Kathy Story:

Kathy is like Jesus. We love Kathy Melissa. Jesus says we are two, first and second. Jesus said, "My life was okay. I want people to feel my pain. I help worse people. I was left out because I did steal food and went to jail. It made me feel stupid and I did bad things after that. I love the Lord. I was Christed at 17. I foresaw some stuff. I kind of like a psychic."

He said the best time of his life was when he married a close relative of Kathy's. He says they had two children at that time. He says he also loved his mother in the first life, but he wasn't too close to her. He said, "Love is the most positive thing there can ever be, I think." He said his wife in a later life (a life that was better) was Mary and she had beautiful light hair.

Story from the Loving People:

We love Jesus' hair recently. We felt emotion and loved him for feeling so loving and despaired on us he wanted better things for us. He gave many of us the most love or such we ever felt. He gave us the right mate. We knew because he appeared and told us where to go to find love. He told us whom to love and we are all happy. He told us Kathy may help in the 2nd coming and would probably die in a fire at 37 (THIS IS A JOKE I GUESS BECAUSE I'M 60). We don't like his method of helling, he sometimes visions us then melts it. He sometimes tells us we're dying because we did something he didn't like, like spending too much money buying clothes. He loves us because we heaven him.

My Story – Kathy

The first time I came to know Jesus I was in a church, and as I got ready to go to the altar a beautiful ray of light came down from above. I made my way to the altar to accept Jesus as if driven by an invisible force. I was totally sublime, although church did not close as it ordinarily did at 12:00. It didn't even give a recess for Sunday School at 10:45. I felt a little concerned but with my sister and best friend, I made my way to the front of the pews and reached out to a lovely hug from the minister. It was

Kenmore Baptist Church, and I was 12 years old. He told us we were a wonderful example to the Church.

Still, I had not felt what so many refer to as his touch. I waited until I was really 37 and lying out in the back yard. I was thinking about Jesus and his love when I heard a child crying. It touched me so much I prayed for Jesus to help the girl. As the girl stopped crying, I suddenly felt Jesus' pain and tears for the lack of people understanding His life, for the lack of knowing a perfect man. I wanted everyone to know His pain, mostly in the despair that He was alone, misunderstood and among strangers who despised his perfect love. In the years between, I had backslid over a lost love and sought to find another love in so many men. I felt so many rejections because I didn't know too well or stick with a chaste life. I fell to the depths at 27 when I developed a sad disease. And it was in and out of the Clinic several times. Each time I told myself I wanted no more backsliding with men. But somehow the lack of affection drove me to be with several more men for a hopeful Love. Love didn't come for years, but one day I met a wonderful man. I still made the mistake of asking the man almost right at first sight, not letting him find me as the Bible says. But Roger knew the Lord and had an ear to Jesus. After many months of loving, he told me Jesus loved me but I had loved so many men that he was quite displeased with me. I vowed to trust that and felt much better about my holiness. I really felt Jesus loved me for coming to me through Roger, my long-time lover. And I will never forget

Roger nor the love I began to feel for Jesus. Roger told me I also had the gift of healing. I sought to get in touch with Jesus any way I could. Today I have heard him whisper, "I am praying for you," and many other comforting thoughts. Later I learned to ask, and he let me let me have many of these writings.

When I was 37, I felt very unstill inside and without peace. I was crying over lack of much of a life and cried out, "I have no peace!" I fell onto the bed and sobbed until I heard a direct voice saying, "I am Peace" Lord said. He said it with so much feeling that I instantly loved Him. I dedicated my life to serving the Trinity of God (Jesus, Lord, and God).

My family doesn't all go to church but I know my dear sister goes regularly. She studied the Bible and when I think all is lost she reminds me of the Bible's promises. I always feel better when I talk to her.

When my sister and I were small, she led the way and I was always happy to go along to be included. I loved her and felt joy, but a little tired out at keeping up with her. Kathy did however die because she thought there was no good left in the world in 1981. It was a cabin scene, I believe, and I was going to leave my family and fly back to my condo in Sarasota just to rest alone. Of course I can't actually recall this, but it was told to me by genuine people. Kathy was on the brink of losing her mind and found all her old friends and such, up North, to be total lumps without love for anything. She felt she was going out of her mind with ick! They say she was slashed and was spelled back up by God with another soul. But she had gone through a time with an awful, "What?" to any question. She felt depressed and slow. But Kathy does have a rare, above Genius Intelligence Quotient (tested I.Q. number). For a while, she felt so dumb, she laughed hysterically at stupid stuff, and cries out loud, out of control, when she feels injury of any good thing or person. She lost her 'love' mate and he tried to kill her, too.

Ida's loss was in 1988 when she was in her home secure and in came an intruder with a knife. The woman was upset because Ida's daughter was subsisting on bare necessities and not even that. She was outraged that something was not done about the conditions that Miss lived under. She then stabbed Ida in the back and Ida bled till she died. It was a horror to Miss that her mother did this, but something spelled her back up with a worse condition. She was no more love at all for Miss and Miss was in total chaos without even a friend because the intruder, was her friend.

WHAT THE HAPPY PEOPLE, OR US WE, WOULD SAY:

We are happy when we are home safe and our wives do the dishes. We like our wives. Our wives mean everything to us and much love. We do the dishes sometimes. It's nice to be away for a little while but we like to come home. Like . . . sipping wine . . . You know pin wheels make us happy among other simple pleasures. Being with our wives is our only real pleasure. We like also winning something if we're playing a game. We like to speed when we're young. We also like to swim if we

can get to a lake or pool. It's not what we call love but mutual getting along.
If we didn't have a wife we think we would be so sorry; we would have to go out and trap someone else, we would.

We like a clean smell.

About our wives working, well, if she can do it all (not too many can) we think it's okay. We love having a home. If we live in an apartment we feel stupid. We serve Jesus (somebody said that). Every so often we get unseen help.

As we go on here, it's slightly other people. We eat plenty but we don't get fat. We get advice from pictures and voices. We feel very intelligent. We are very loving. We have books that kind of interest us.

LIGHT

People that love are the best people in the world. I want them to be at home.
Knowing is all wonderful. If a voice tells you something, your pretty well have it. The best people got to be loving. Love bounces back to you. Love does come back to you if you let yours show.

SELF

Love is very essential. And I do believe we are a loving people.

I'm worried. I try to do too much. I have opinions and don't want to chill people because of my overt comments. But dilly dallying is a good way to get interrupted and make no comment. People have tried to make oblique comments on my life and they are not true. That's why I don't believe in oblique comments. Really, many of them were trying to be helpful. They were hoping. The knife slices too.

One time I looked as far as I could look and could find no more love in the world. So I prayed to die and felt Jesus would want the world to end. In my heart I didn't want the world to end just now but I prayed I would die. My mother said no, she would go with my father.

I grew love again by studying healing – both by the laying on of hands and by absentee and prayer healing. Many successes and much love. Till it struck again. Got hated certain people and takes their sleep away. Months of it for me. Evil doctors. No medicine for it from them folks, no.

Now it's hard to find much love. I quiver inside and out. Somebody recently healed me of the insomnia, but such a heart – it pulsates. Such quivers.

I have found that people will usually provide what I need if I ask. And finally I'm not afraid to ask anymore. But there's no more hell to do to someone than no more sleep. Hell is. Restorill does help. Unfortunately until doctors read my other book, they would not prescribe it to mental clients. At the time I needed it the medical doctor would prescribe it, but only for a while. Also at the time, unfortunately the mental health doctors gave me pills that caused insomnia and made me quiver.

I go to church and pray, but I sometimes don't have anything to offer them. They'd like me to sing in the choir but I can't ad lib it. I would like to help. I do know about deities and God of the World. He is quite a beauty.

Love is essential. We are a loving people. Love is of God. When God hates a person, he does not let them love. Sometimes God says something through a person to stop them from loving. God tells them what to say. When your love is gone you can pray to the Lord for your love back. I love the Lord. We all need love. God is all knowing. He judges and wants to help even the people he only likes. Keep in the will of God or the Lord, hoping and trying to do better.

Love is of God. Plan a life that will let God have an ideal through you. No matter what you've done or tried and failed (as I have) you have to have a plan that you think is just great, ask God to put his approval on it. He will let you know.

He may let a special person in your life ask you some questions and you will feel good about what you have let him know about your plan. He will be mostly like a friend. Let him know your plan.

God, everyone did let us live. We love him for this. If we are "marshmallow" or marshmallow-type, very nice and sweetest, it is hard for God to love you. He sees that children who are spit fires and very adorable have vision. They can be angry and mean and often hate filled. But they are angry, you see. They can't feel love as much as their sweetest counterparts.

We believe these spit-fires have love but may have difficulty with people who love more. My darling sister was a spit-fire and like a pops-a-ball just keeps going. I am very proud of her and all her accomplishments. But I cannot live with her. The old way, you see, where she used to scream at me over make-up, blacken my eye for the first day of high school, or pee on me during the night and kick me so hard I was black and blue. God plans to help everybody. If you have been a cushion as a young person, be angry enough at yourself to become a little bit of a spit-thing. There's more, but it's a little further on.

Believe in God. There's nothing more stupid than a cushion. Live for something, or you'll just be a hangin'-on marshmallow and fall for anything.

If you never get visions, you have to keep trying. I write. People who tread eagerly and spit fire get God to help them. He usually lets their father or a close uncle or such give them "slides" – a future. The patty-cake gets crap. Only, -- one way out. Have it out with God. Let him lead you. Psychics are usually a trouble for these types of people. The message often gets struck down. God is usually nearby, however. Get a good message from round about. I see pictures and hear a small voice to get a message.

I'm feeling troubled though. I don't have all the answers.

Please answer me God. I feel I'm having all kinds of problems and I'm praying for love. I live with my family but they won't make time for me except to correct me. I'm 37.

God loves me. I thought about getting a bumper sticker that said, "God Likes Me." If he does, I like him. I feel good about striking out. I don't really have an ornery child to hell this out on, so I just use God. I know he thinks I'm a fudge, but angry because even so I'm a good heart. I never hurt anyone, and always try to be compassionate. I like the motto, "Ours is to help and not to hurt." I think everyone should adopt this motto, and we would be a better world. God must know I am not evil. God is love. I am ONLY that, but can't go about the next step.

I have never been led into a relationship by God. I've used the Cave Girl Approach of clamoring in and landing my prey. It always got away from me, too.

I bought a cat and saved one at the Animal Shelter. Such a good thing that I bought Smokie (new name Porkie) because Mom gave the other one (Misty) away when we moved. She wouldn't give away something that cost a great deal of money. Now I have very little on my agenda, very little to love that is.

When I laugh I feel love. God is sometimes hard on me. Earrings break in my hands. Sunglasses disappear. Just bought. Several good pairs of shoes all gone. I feel like crying. I guess many people do. They probably strike out and hurt something. I hurt myself inside.

I went to the doctor about my insomnia. He read what the other doctor had prescribed. Restorill and Lithium. "Can't have it," he said. I argued for a while, and finally yelled. He yelled back and asked me to go outside and wait. I really let him have it. I waited for a while but felt certain he was going to put me in a mental ward. So I left and went to the Mall. When I got home, the doctor and my mother had sent for the paddy wagon. Off to a mental hospital I went. Four days no sleep. Restorill prescribed. There were two doctors just slightly names changed but the face was almost the same. Very nice. Released.

Mom locked me upstairs and made an appointment with the first doctor I had been ripped to shreds by. The nice hospital doctor told me to see the other doctor and the same agency. But mother wants terror in my heart I guess. Now I have that appointment to look forward to.

When Mom was feeling good about me she actually did say, "I'll leave it to you whether you want any more doctors or not." I was prepared to say no. She can't remember that now.

I really love her. But I found a duplex in Fairlawn for $150 a month. Mother made me stay with her for most of my money.

Truth is all I lean on. Injustice is everywhere. It nearly killed me.

Please remember to try to trap your love. If you blurt out a sentence and lose your love, pray. The Lord is very good And don't let any kid be a pancake. We all want a love in the family, it's true. But get them interested in a chore they might enjoy.

Please tell me Bible stories. I have been saved and went to Sunday School for years. But memory is bad. I pray it will get better. Well, for me, and the love that I express to all the world I need a little pear juice now, apple juice. I need love. I love God. God is.

(end of Self material)

Churches and Denominations

Any church is a good church. We have denominations because people do have a tendency to pick things apart. Lord is in a good church. Churches that have a good sound to their name are usually good. Like Kenmore Baptist Church. Unity Church of Akron.

In churches, women are really expected to be good listeners. Pray for the men at the pulpit. Don't be the attention there. People, if you go to a church for the good-looking women like the soloist or singing trios and such – evil.

Right now about the Spiritual churches. If you go to one at this time you can expect to wait a few years (written in 1991) for anything nice.

It's the people that make the church.

Prayer is such a good thing. If you meet on prayer night, always have something to pray for. Praying for your loved ones is a good thing.

In a church where you've been helped, you should say thank you before going on. But testimonials are less than purposeful.

Church is for the study, and it should be the scripture and certain books that help or relate. Church is also for prayer. And it is for communion and deities. I feel choirs should be omitted (Lord God) and music is not for church. Some people like it.

Changing churches is not a good thing, because the people that helped you get started are not there anymore.

Sex And What It Means

I would have sex with a partner if I loved him. If you don't love the partner you get evil from him. Sex with me is beautiful. Like the man and he'll like you. We all have sex to have love. Almighty says it tames you. Almighty says it helps you. Men may need sex a few times in a day. They like it hard. Women need to develop their sexuality. They dream of love to do this. They should enjoy sex maybe two times a day. This is for people who want sex. If you don't have a man, God will get you one if you have "It."

Religions

Ours and All Others. (So as also concerning the sexuality) Ours is Christian. We mean you shouldn't have sex unless you are married. If you are religious this means you. If you do have sex before marriage you can still get married. In all other religions marriage is not required. They mean you don't have to love God. They have goddess or priestess and she gives sex for a blessing. It cleanses a man. In our religion we believe love happens to a man. And man makes the first move. If the woman makes the first move she gets evil. Love is when a man knows. We believe love should be happening. It should boil when it boils. Usually about two weeks. If it's love and you get married you're happy. If you hate him for some reason after marriage, then divorce. He hates you, you know, because you are not loving. Let's hope for love. If they have a loving wife, they can have oral sex.

Drugs

Drugs are sort of good. We learn. We learn a little. Cocaine can mess you up but it used to be legal syrup to ease depression. Dr. Sigmund Freud supported Cocaine, but people over used it so he later reneged on his idea. Everything in moderation. Hash cleanses. I like hash. Cities where pot is hammered are stealth. Cleveland somewhat. They hammer pot there. If they leave it alone we'll let them be okay. Cities like Detroit are good. Look out for cities like Hammond, Indiana. Ghosttowns are good. Look out for Danville, Indiana. Georgia is good. West Point is good. Maine is nearly god, very good. Utah? Spain is good. Florida is good and good for the market. Jupiter is good. Monte Carlo is good. Hate is bad. January is a good month. Evil is March. A letter is "L."

Drugs and Alcohol

Alcohol makes you think you're great. Alcohol makes your ticker race. If you drink alcohol you usually like yourself. Ladies may be graceful to drink it but God lets them to have a good time. I really think it's only good in moderation because nobody should have a great deal. Chewing tobacco is very good. Calms you like a baby.

Leadership Transcript

Kathy was born with the best of L in her. Like her love for herself, her beauty was there too. Her policy of being accurate. Her chastity. Her being. Her pleasure with herself. Her melding with others. Her likeableness. Her angelic qualities. Her posture. Her way of saying, "I love you." Her sense of knowing about people and whom to trust. Her divinity. Her level headedness.

Someone in Kathy's family acting as God over her took that away from her. And he said someone else should have it. The person who got it and was original turned some of those qualities into evil, but mainly turned into a very good person and is helping Kathy now.

Kathy got no qualities in return for losing hers, and whatever happened happened.

The person who got Kathy's qualities from her during her young years had a lot of hate. Kathy learned to love a lot because she was a very good heart. But Kathy had a lot of injustices done to her. She still has a good love but not the love of the World. Her life is a memoir.

This sounds kinds of nuts but Kathy's brain type material was eviled out at a very low cost hospital in the state of Ohio. Everybody is trying to hurt her, but it's really about 15 percent. They are traitors.

When the girl that got Kathy's qualities was born, she was a difficult child. She hated her mother and many people. But Kathy's qualities made her truly beautiful. Kathy Tyrity has a K but it was made for her by the man in the family; she's an L in spirit.

THE SIMPLE LIFE . . .

The world may be in shambles here and there. We don't want to say it. Anyway we think true love is the only way to keep people united. They cannot fly through space and time if someone needs them. We want all God's creatures to start making families. The best life for all is the simple life. A home. Two children. A wife to make meals and they should be thought out.

THE ASPECT OF CHILDREN

We want children. Especially the beautiful talented women. They are our best asset. The black people have been given the idea. Let's even up. We want more ladies of creation. Let's be a team and share the world together. God of Love. We want the children so our world can go on. There were many spelled up to leave in God's name.

CHANNELLING

It is a rare gift. Those predisposed to it have red hair or dark hair, and some other colors. If you channel you should use the Lord's power of protection. Say a prayer, and use the Lord's name. He likes to give his protection. Channeling is for getting the Universe to give messages. We hope we can save the world. It's a talent that is given only to adepts. They have a rare insight. We hope we can save the world. We channel the Holy Ghost and God power through Miss Kathy M. Tyrity.

GAMES OF CHANCE

There are a few but we play only Lotto: the numbers to play are 10, 17, 19, 23, 18, 25. The games of chance are winning games and they play a lot of sleepiness for Kathy.

THE PLANETS

There will be no severe changes. A light will come down from space and tell us the future. That's Aries. That's all.

(END OF CHAPTER)

NEXT: SPIRITUAL REALITY TEACHING

A Spiritual Reality Teaching

Bill of Rights, Article #1 – freedom of religion

Fortune telling is illegal in some states; but legal in connection with religious.

....

Bible 1 – great religions all right

New Testament – Love and forgiveness

1 Corinthians Ch. 12 #7 – Everybody has a psychic spirit.

Christian and scientific:

Three S's in Psychic Development—

1) Safe – psychic laws (possession by spirit)

2) Sane – no fanatics – delusions

3) Scientific – prove the reality of Psychic principle

Right motive – can be used for good or bad

Spirituality minded interest in truth.

Cleanliness, patience, don't demand results, or any kind of gift.

System for 3 S's: You're the boss of Self.

Atonement – prepare the body, relax; faith makes all possible.

***Use steps for meditation 15 minutes, twice a day.

Light surrounds the whole room – hands on thighs or loosely together; raise head slightly.

Unaware of physical body – look at candle flame or close your eyes.

Healing movements --- I can show you these in a video or class.

Spiritual Healing

Of the Spirit, not through the spirit.
God is the one and only healer – eternal physician.

Benefits:

1) Self healing, daily renewal plan

2) Healing practitioner

Ways of healing:

1) Instant

2) gradual recovery

Feelings:

1) warm, hot

2) pulsation beat

3) electrical feeling

to RESTORE harmony of body – health harmony of soul is – happiness.

Harmony in nature is often – disturbed.

Health, happiness, holiness – have harmony.

   1) outer man

   2) spiritual, mental environment – inner war.

Faith binds healer and God.

Stronger faith works best – instant.

Healers – faith could do it.

1) religious laws

2) man's laws

a) Give God credit!

b) proper setting – white candle.

3) method –

a) lift and touch into positions
b) don't touch below the shoulders except back

Auric treatment – below shoulders

3 inches from aura or area – no diagnosis or prescribe anything.

No mechanical devices – vibrators

No psychic energy (faith works) and no phonies

Magnetic healing by touch – everyone has it.

Used by animals instinctively – Gift of God to all living Creatures.

They lie close to stricken creature

Breathe on area; stroking.

Ancient China and Egypt. Jesus used touch and prayer.

Frederick Mesner 200 years ago a Mesmerizing Vienese doctor, of around 1778.

Vital fluid universal – animal magnetism. In man's body.

Proved it can be transferred one body to another by means of touching or passes.

Curative – is sleeping to relieve pain.

Also produce trance. NOT hypnotism.

Physiological not psychological.

Vital fluid is like current (force) directed by willpower, free will
Self healing and all, power varies.

Small percentage of natural born healers.

Law of use – the more you use your healing power, the more and more healing power you will have to use.

HOW TO DEVELOP:

1) The WILL to heal
2) Stimulate desire
3) Stimulate the health of the healers
4) Proper rest, sleep and diet.
5) Do you breathing exercises.
6) avoiding indulgences
7) Personal effort and positive attitude

8) Daily quiet period.

Healer: try to work with self

1) Ask guides' assistance. Surround yourself from the top of your head -- shower the inner brain with water like a big geyser washing out your inner head. Raise your hands, fill them with light. Project it from tips of fingers – and heal in the name of Jesus.

2) Principal of harmony – Relax……. Open to the

flow of energy – directed by will.

HEALING TREATMENT

1) opening the way

2) directing in curative magnetic flow

3) draw out all inharmony

Source of Magnetism – stored in body in psychic center.

Notes

1) God is the one and only healer. I am an instrument, channel, I desire to be used for service.

2) Step left. Right hand on base of the neck, left hand on forehead

3) Move from head to crown

4) 3 movements across back – right, middle, left, and back to the middle

5) Put hand near chest and heart, about 3 inches away

In the name of the father
And through the son
And by the holy spirit

Breathing – Hindus – India

Prayer – spontaneous healing – oldest form

India – science is religion
   Soul science, pranic breathing
   Disease practically unknown

PREVENTIVE practice

Nervous disorders almost nonexistent
West – over 50 percent of all disease
Health depends on correct breathing
Slowest breathing animals live longest
Mental health greatly affected
CNS (central nervous system) connects with breathing.
Fear, anger, peace – going to sleep

Breathing follows thought – take deep breath

PRANA – absolute energy – in air charge

Carried to nervous system

Storehouse – solar plexus – radiates through nervous system.

Breathe like going to sleep.

PSYCHICS NEED CONTROL IN STUDIES AND PROCEDURES

Safe and Sane – Strong power – atom bomb

Can't fool God. Keep a psychic journal

Events and happenings, visions voices

Control your tongue, bless and curse not.

Mastery of the tongue

*developed controlled psychic

Natural born sensitive has "open doors" which tend to possess body and mind

Harassed by evil spirit – could be exorcized

Don't play with Ouiju Board – invites negative spirits

Spirit can come any time to natural psychic

Can't progress

Listen and practice and you will grow

1) Earth teacher

2) Spirit teacher – revealed to you

Co-partner – 15 minutes limit on meditation, twice a day if you like.

Psychometry – soul measuring – mental phenomenon (holding keys or watch or metal from another person to stare into their future.)

John 4:7 example of psychometry – water bowl

Acts 21: 10 & 11 Paul's belt and Agabus

1) Letters – remove from envelope

Hold in hands – happy sad, worried, good news, etc. you feel it

Hold letter to nerve centers – read letter

Open awareness

2) Phone – who is it?
The law of vibration figures most prominent in all phases of mediumship mental or physical. The law of use. The more you use your intuitive psychic awareness, the better it gets.

3) Ask in your 15 minute meditation for something personal
a) Don't need to ask more questions

INVOCATION

1) Psychic awareness opening

"I now open my psychic awareness. I am open to the good and closed to the ill. Deep within me, I place a psychic barrier, so that if anything of an undesirable nature should touch me, the psychic energy will be broken instantly. This is my psychic prayer of protection." Say this and memorize it.

2) Psychic Law of Protection, spreading the white light all around you, your co-partner and the room. Lighting 4 white

candles, open bible, incense burning and a kettle of cool water on the floor. Can use red candles for love or green for prosperity, or blue for spirit. The bright magenta candles are for transformations throughout the winter Solstice. Green can also be for healing.

3) The Attunement procedure. Ring a soft glass bell a few times or brass, porcelain or whatever.

Look at the candle flame until you can see it with eyes closed. See an image in your third or central eye. Practice meditation and meditation prayers. Pray to God in all practicality. Listen to your teacher. Look up at her or him. Stare at their eyes and listen. Do as the book says and the teachers all say about the same type of prayer.

3) The half hour Psychic Meditation. Sit in a chair in a circle with the other students and one teacher. Your feet flat on

the floor. Posture straight and low steady breathing. Hands on your knees or thighs, palms up. Close your eyes and see a beach scene with cresting waves, birds, beauty and soft, damp golden sand as you walk. Your father, grandfather, mother or such in spirit may appear to you there and talk to you. It's nice. Walk along and you may find another teacher to impart wisdom. God of Knowledge and

Wisdom is for those who seek Truth, Knowledge and Awareness, psychic energy. He is beyond belief to look at. Beyond knowledge itself. Talk to God of Truth and Knowledge. He will let you know something.

4) Continue with the psychic meditation. See all you can this time, with eyes shut. Meditate on wonderful beautiful scenes, a bouquet of flowers, or sometimes a mother's love. Later you

can see the pure action of Spirit with your eyes open. Practice looking at a sheet of white paper on the table. Each of you see a picture there and describe it. Then practice going around the room and everybody give everybody else a psychic message. Get some for yourself too. Then as you progress you may use a white painted wall to glare at or even images in the room or in the person's natural aura about them. See the colors of their aura and tell it to them, eyes open. As you progress you will see more. Now close. Pull a streak of white light down around the head and over the back. Say, thank you to your guides and loved ones and also the Teacher.

5) Benediction: "I now close my psychic awareness. May the Lord watch between me and Thee while we are apart, one from another. Amen." And if you are trying to sleep take one

or two helpful self pulling up messages then say, "God, take it away and may I sleep 8 hours." You should sleep 11 to 7.

(TAKE A BREAK)

3/18/1986

Psychometry – 85% is good percentage in mediumship.

Psychic Center becomes more acute; handshake, hug.

Place hands over hands – telepathic link between medium, object and owner.

Hints: 1) Try to relax. 2) Be alert; open. 3) Note feelings, mental impressions

Readings through mail – cut hair behind ear…2 envelopes. (watch out for phony animal hair). Gets what he deserves.

Job 4-15 accuracy – hair of flesh stood up.

....

March 25

Seeing pictures is clairvoyance in psychometry.

Or, it is **CLEAR SEEING**.

Signs of Clairvoyance – burning in eyes

- perceptions of lights, visions or rolling vapor.

Another form of Psychic Contact with the world of spirit is simple Automatic Writing. Take a felt tip pen and large sheet of paper. Spirit operators will decide the work. Hold the pen to the paper lightly; write your name, ask for a spiritual guide to fill in a sentence or two.

Yet another form of contact is development of Inspirational Writing – feeling of bright light over shoulder……..can even develop into Inspirational Speaking.

Wake up with an idea or get it in trance state.

HOMEWORK – bring forward. The automatic sketching or writing. Any Inspirational writing or speaking. Learn those.

•••

DREAMS

April 6, 1986 dream: 1) agenda of 'readers' to go to bed with in groups of 7 beds. No actual sex. 2) Preparing for a huge dinner for friend Greer who was supposed to help me with dessert. Hot moist white towels were brought also to the table. 3) Went to New York City – had more fun on the bowery than on Park Ave. – with mother, climbed the roof of a beautiful blue building and roller skated down the other side. Barely made it to the peak. Back home, entertained a professional ball team and played matchmaker with the girls in the community.

Also dreamed of healing my father's hands and telling Steve I would not marry him, which I didn't.

....

April 8, Class. Try Automatic Writing again. Seclusion is best.

Auras – Energy field surrounding every living thing.

Aura enfolds you like an eggshell. It is protection from curiousity and against lower vibration spirits; doesn't mean you are bad, good, or whatever.

But the WHITE, GOLD aura is very spiritually evolved. Goes around the whole body.

Auras do CHANGE from time to time. Size depends on vitality. Health tells in the aura. Attitude and character tells. Human aura appears to be white but it is not. (energy field, is a white mist). Color is seen in the aura. Luminous vapor pulsating or gently moving. Only look when open psychic awareness. Could get unbalanced. Up one day, down the next; positive & negative spirit talking all the time. "I am not open," tell them. "Please wait. Come back when I am open." Only accept the message in an

emergency. Rays may flash, spiral or projecting, in Energetic people. Open awareness for church. Sickness is caused by inharmony. Reharmonize your vibration for healthy day. Healings are much help, too. Magnetic touch laying on of hands helps so much. Direct contact floods entire being…..visualize light going in. Know and feel you are being healed, or that you are giving a proper healing, too. Spirit will guide you. Keep visualizing. What makes it work – by willing it. Some are natural healers – a pat or close contact; but the desire to heal makes twice as strong the intended healing for people or animals.

Control your aura. Against illness and ill feelings. Control by your will. 1) Expand – blend with other people, pick up feelings. 2) contract back in the eggshape of your own aura to protect. But when a person is truly being affectionate, the aura does expand.

This is why a husband, loved one, or wife can hurt you more.

4) depression – aura expands. 4) Contract – when frightened; or when you don't like someone.

Picture your aura expanding and contracting. Want to expand around a circle of interesting friends while communicating. Should like the others in your learning circle. Contract the aura when going near sickness or depression so you won't absorb it.

See the Aura:

1) When you are alone

Who are you   Who's with you

2) Uria first

3) Surround car and self with light

4) Are you Same Dr. Forrest

5) Are you Same Dr. J

Salmony pink color in Aura means good health

DREAM April 25 – Paper mache teddy bear turned out to be a child's train ? I squeeze it sitting behind a lot of paper – The doctor next to me said, "Now, I'll have to do something to fix that; what'll I do – You weren't supposed to move the train. (Later the result happened in Barstow).

- Songs I dreamed of "Smoke on the Water, fire in the sky." "Watch the bridges ever burning. Don't say a word about tomorrow or forever. There'll be time enough for sadness when you leave me." And, "Make believe you love me one more time." "Jump In" the bay. Salt water.

- ALSO April 25 – a) Unknown doctor gave me a shot b) Apartment first floor, right end, spirits gave gifts. First the men – black wrought iron box, ZING with the fingers. Bamboo fixtures on wall, lit inside. Big, lit aquarium, big fish. Front panel of apartment large sliding glass doors. All my friends washed them. One lady gave me a navy blue gro-grain ribbon THIN for a bow in my hair.

b) first dream. The ladies who came were Marcia and Cindy and others. April 28, dreamed I was summoned for jury duty on Shirley Quick murder trial, 4:00 courthouse.

....

1) Strict control – limit psychic work to 15

minutes. Not too many teachers, One.

May 13 – Third Eye
SYMBOLS

MOST OF WHAT YOU SEE WILL BE SYMBOLS

There is a key to interpreting.

With every symbol, there is a threadlike attachment with the symbol.

THREAD IS INTERPRETATION. In other words, an **ACCOMPANYING IMPRESSION** clothes a symbol. It is fragile, may escape recognition. It is a personal skill.

> a) Picture Comes – Pause – silently inquire – **WHAT IS SYMBOL'S MEANING?**
>
> b) Distorted Symbol meaning – **ALWAYS HOLD TO FIRST IMPRESSION**

2 kinds of symbols

Universal Symbols with definite meaning.

CROSS - RELIGION
SCHOOL - EDUCATION

TEARS – SORROW

OPEN HAND – FRIENDSHIP

LETTER – NEWS (or by telephone) – communication

Fixed Symbols – fixed to the psychic

WHITE SATIN – spiritual state, purity, wedding

HEAVY SMELL OF ROSES – coming death – or beautiful feeling, whichever it is to you.

DOCTOR --- Illness, Physical condition

RAT – Unpleasant personal condition

SYMBOL PROJECTION – Why is it done? Economical in psychic energy.
A picture's worth a thousand words.

Personal intimate nature – so given in good taste

....

Unlimited Symbol Meanings

Portray any situation

- basic meaning – no minor details. A SYMBOL REPRESENTS. AN IMAGE IS A REPRODUCTION

Summary: A symbol represents something but the meaning is general – feeling adds the message   or

Picture that's not a symbol – could be an IMAGE a church, a bible

IMAGE is a Reproduction – something MEANINGFUL TO THE PERSON – ASK FOR FURTHER IMAGE OR FEELING – woman, love, mother
IF RISING HAS A VOID – ABSENCE OF MEANING – IT'S AN IMAGE. Only occasionally is an image gathered.

Stop and silently inquire
What is the meaning of this symbol.

....

Back to the colors of the Aura

Gray – negative or depressed

White – very high, rare

Blue – devotional, mental

Pink – good cheery and good health, loving

Yellow – intellect

Red – energetic, out-going – If it is dark and dingy, lust and sensual nature. With blackish red – rape or murder. Stay away

---

Three Levels Or Degrees Of Reading Auras

a) Seeing white

    b) See size and contours
    c) Symbols – transfigurations

Spirit may speak in languages.

Symbol – white horse – love of animals

Image – white horse – father's prize white horse

Symbol – Ask – What is meant by this symbol.

    Thought may come to mind.

A distorted symbol may come about if you stop to reason it out.

--you're just a channel

Distorted images – vision of Jesus – a symbol, means higher enlightenment

*trance

A form of allowing spirit to speak through you.

May 28 dream – got to a special party with rip in dress and tennis shoes which were off – asked to leave the opera - no ride home. Saw cities which were being demolished.

---

5 physical senses and 5 super normal channels

1) Eye   * Clairvoyance – 3rd eye

2) Ear   * Clairaudience

3) Nose   * Clairsentance

4) Mouth   * Clair savourance --- taste.

5) Feeling   * Clair sensuousness

Physical Phenomenon

Trumpet, levitation, apport work.

In the old-fashioned sensitive parties they used a form of trumpet. Even in my day, levitation parties showed how that works. Apports work – article manifests – gems, rose, wheat – may be transparent or not solid but can be real (often phony or staged). I have had many real apports and love them all the time.

The next two helps require patience and conditions – can be observed by other people. The difference is, if it is PHYSICAL, ectoplasm (teleplasm) is used – excretion from body. Some have more of it, but all have some. If you sit long enough (years) you will see something happen. May be extracted from sitters as well as mediums. topening or lights in the ends of fingers (strings) white stuff. MOVE SLOWLY in a circle. If I'm there or trance, don't touch me or turn on light.

June 17, 1986

Matthew 3:16 Mat. 1:20 Mat. 20: 1-5, Mat.17: 1-3; Mat. 2 – 13.

DREAMS – 3 Kinds.

    1) physical – causal factors – vitamins, food, heart works harder

    2) psychological dream – mental factor relating – worry about

someone or thoughts about them, someone attracted to you, chased, healthy to dream, everyone dreams.

3) Psychic Dream – spontaneous Symbols may recur, warning . . . solution, etc. – will be confirmed by earthly events later.

- Need control – No way to control

- Read Matt. 2:13 & 14 and Genesis 41: 17-32 and 37: 5-9.

Your Psychic Dream will be meaningful – with message for you

Short revealment – symbols may recur – something "hot"

A warning may say don't go on trip; car not safe.

Solutions offered after request "What can I do?"

Visitation from someone in spirit by Earthly dreamer.

Generally, can verify psychic events

Premonitions to occur even in dreams.

HOW TO EXPERIENCE A PSYCHIC DREAM:

1) When in meditation, ask spirit friends. Affirm that you are open to psychic susceptibility.
2) Almost always a seeing experience, you're not talking.

3) Will be confirmed by earthly events.

4) A different feel about them

5) Usually so you can help outcome

6) Travel to other dimensions

7) Dream into past life

8) Note: astral body always leaves sleeper.

Universal Church of the Master
7/1

We want to be accurate
But it's difficult – another dimension

Trance – the spirit must study you to take over

Mediumship – can take years

Ego can be a problem – confidence will come with experience and knowledge.

1) Don't let subconscious give you messages. Psychic energy may be worn out. Psychic energy. "Head messages" wrong. Don't hold on to messages. Done and forgotten. Don't rationalize or think it over. Don't go to friends all the time to give a message in Church (metaphysical or spiritual church of the master). Go to someone you don't know. Don't say the same things other psychics said.

Nobody is 100 percent accurate. Can misinterpret. The most difficult thing is messages for self. We are of service. We humble ourselves. We Best workers don't thrive on Ego. You are a channel and can lose it. *Don't make big predictions with dates absolute. Time means nothing – hard to predict. Remain well-balanced. Destiny will help you make it. Shine light to dark corridors of self. Am I dedicated?

Examine yourself. Never make something up.

2) Don't try to blank your mind out
3) Relax physical body

May the group sing: "Words of Life," "Hallelujah" and "Only Believe."

Noises, voices: you have protection. Sit still – no fast moves in meditation ever; never grab or flash light. Light or dead sleep state (very rare) deep state very dangerous. Nothing should disturb them . . . In trance state, it is a gentle fusing or blending of personalities. When a spirit is coming through to you, you trance as a healer.

Bodily habits influence development -- *moderation. Spirit operators draw impurities from aura to develop. Good – not good enough. We want the best. Changes in body due to aura changes; need self control.

Cold shudders, heat, drowsiness, hepped up, discomfort, tummy-heartbeat, head throat, moodiness, emotional stimulation, up and down. Development puts strain on nerves.

WHY SO SLOW DEVELOPMENT

--There are changes in your glands – can't rush laws of nature.

Mark 4:28 – all growth due in time *Sept. 2 Astral Travel – we all do it while sleeping, seems wonderful – little trips. HOW TO DO IT Consciously – safe and easy to achieve, takes practice – do it in light or dark (*use etheric light – from fingertips – to see.) See and hear the same but those in physical body can't see or hear you. You THINK yourself here and there. Can leave body if there is a threat to it (rape, murder, etc.) like flying or floating. Visit others to do HEALING – can't lift anything. No one else sees your light in the darkness.

SEPTEMBER 16, 1986 – Last Class.

Astral Travel.

To move our awareness (that sees, hears and feels). Use protection prayer….floating, flying.

Invisible and weightless – go through walls and many miles.

Could automatically return – little shock. No harm will befall you in astral body.

1) Could be led on 'drug trip'
2) Someone else could enter your body.

Companion (spirit) in sleep protection to you, release, escape.

Educational:

Tell your guides you want to remember and need their protection.

We always travel on our level.

1) Get a "scene" picture – (no water) 6 feet away
2) Relax, open awareness - attunement.
3) Look at scene 5 minutes – think about details and surroundings
4) Close eyes and still see it.

Sit close – then back off and remember close feeling.

5) Pretend standing up and walking cross floor to picture.

6) Pretend set your self in front of picture.

After you do these steps casually, you will begin to leave your body at some point. It comes slowly and some people can do it only in a reclining and almost sleep-like condition. But with patience you will learn to do it at will. I have visited other planets, places I've never been on earth, palaces, and the future and future possibilities, all in my future in my life. I think you can too. God be with you and the Holy Ghost.

These messages are for you to begin to develop the

Holy Ghost, God Power and Angels to give messages in your parish. And for you possibly to be a healer. I pray you can do both. Thank you and please go on to the next reading about the Scriptures.

Scriptures

Rev. 15: 2-4 Victory Song

   Oh give thanks unto the Lord for his love endureth forever.
   Sing for all victories. Sing and Say, "I believe you're seeing us/me through."

Pray on knees at night for the lost soul.

Now: John, Mark – A jew, Roman citizen.

Mother wealthy – Mary. Had a Greek servant girl. Acts 12:13.
Home used as a gathering place for Christmas after Pentecost (Apostolic Group).

He fled at the time of Christ's betrayal.
He was a cousin of Barnabas (wealthy Levite From Cyprus island).

Peter lived with Mark and brought him to
Christ.
He was an Early Church member writing a
Book.

Paul and Barnabas visited Jerusalem with an offering for the needy. They met Mark, brought him to Antioch on their return. (Acts 13:5 – Mark Went with Paul and Barnabus on their first missionary journey. Mark was to instruct the new converts.

AT PERGA

Mark went no further probably because he disliked taking gentiles into the Church.

Paul disagreed being a true missionary.

Peter and Mark were friends. They were with Paul in Rome.

Mark traveled widely benefiting him to write to a large audience.

Mark was led by Peter and Paul to picture Christ as the Mighty Servant. Mark then went to Alexandria where he founded the Church. And he became its first Bishop.

He may have been martyred in 62 A.D., the 8th year of Nero's reign.

Mark hurries in breathlessly to shout out the news to all the world – Mathew marched in with regal bearing. Peter – colorful writer, big fisherman; snaps with action all through the Gospel.

Mark and Peter were friends. They both quote the same verse in Mark 1:3 and 1st Peter 24 and 25.

Mark's gospel was written in Rome after the death of Paul and before the fall of Jerusalem A.D. 60.

It was the first gospel written – Mathew and Luke second.
Mattew quoted extensively in the Old Testament.
Mark used Mark 1:2 and 3.
Mark had gentiles in mind.

(absence of Jewish scripture or law) He was writing to Romans to show them Jesus was the servant sublime.

(Mathew and Luke record Jesus' birth but Mark has him as a man) –

John stresses Jesus' pre-existence.

Mark symbol: Ox – Issaih's vision. Ch. 53. Mark shows Christ fulfilled this.

    1) Throngs of people
    2) 19 miracles
    3) 4 parables

4) Healings regarding the demon-possessed

Bustle and activity

Deals with Jesus' Galilian ministry – slight mention of Perean and Judean

To minister and to give his life – John and Jesus

1: 1-13 Servant presented.

1:14 10:52 servant at work.

Christ's ministry cleansed from inner pollution – water for outer sing, fire for inner sins. Abiding and permanent.

Devil equals Accuser

Satan equals Adversary

1:14 to 7:23 – E. Galilee

7:24 – 9:50 – N. Galilee

10:1-52 – Perea and Judea

11:1 to 15:47 – sacrificed

16: 1-20 – Raised to life

(space for notes on scripture)

He cannot heal who has suffered much. For only Sorrow, sorrow understands. They will not come for healing at our touch Who have not seen the scars upon our hands. – Edwin McNeill Poteat

Temptation – Hebrews 4:15 to 10:52

Servant At Work – 1:14 to 10:52

He didn't run from danger – He moved right into the danger zone. Herod – who killed John – lived in Galilee. Jesus is the first preacher 1:14 secondly the miracle worker.
*REPENTANCE MUST PRECEDE BELIEF (baptism by fire mentioned which Kathy had, believe me). The men now called had been disciples of John – known Christ 1 year.

"A Life's Call: 1:16 -19

Was John murdered before Jesus picked his disciples? What was Mark martyred with – What does that mean? (Kathy was touched by a white dove that disappered in her bedroom). To me, the dove meant Christ which means love. Jesus was even christed with a dove on the beach.

After this "test" Jesus made his way from Judea to Galilee.

Christ had a perfect spiritual balance in His life – after strenuous activity he retired for prayer (10 scriptures to this).

"I will be thou clean or In the name of God heal." How often, perhaps our lack of quick obedience has shut us away from many of the healing helps of God!.

Jesus showed power in Galilee (1ˢᵗ tour) over Satanic and physical affliction. Now he looks at sin which is at the base of all other ills.

*THE CARE OF THE HOME, THE CULTURE OF THE BODY, MUST ALWAYS BE SECONDARY TO THE WELFARE OF THE SOUL.

He drew Levi, son of Alphaeus, at Capernaum.

Why Jesus ate with the publicans and sinners:
They that are whole have no need of the physician, but they that are sick – he came not to call the righteous but the sinner to repentance.

New wine must be put into new bottles.

The Son of Man is Lord also of the Sabbath.

*GIVE TO GOD THE BEST HOURS OF THE DAY AND HE WILL HELP YOU IN THE WORST HOURS.

As demon possession showed the tyranny of evil, so leprosy pictures defilement of evil Whose faith is conspicuous in the healing recorded in 2:5 ?
THE FAITH OF FRIENDS.

Matthew – original name Levi – a publican or receiver of "custom" with Rome.

Satan is too smart to undo his own work – Mark 3:23 – 26.

The sower – needs firm soil.

*NEED PATTERN OF CONDUCT – RULES FOR LIVING – CARELESS HABITS CAN BECOME THE MASTERS THAT WILL DRIVE OUT THE LAST VESTIGE OF RELIGIOUS FAITH.

Mark 4:7, 18 – 19. I Cor. 9, 25 – 27.

NEED CONVICTIONS THAT GRIP – NOT ONLY EMOTIONS.

"When I am sore beset I seek some quiet place; some lonely room or barren, wind-swept hill, And there in silence wait alone until I see again the smile upon God's face. – I feel his presence fill me like the dawn. And hear once more his whispered, "Peace, be still," And know again the strength to do His will. I turn to take my load and find it gone."

Antoinette Goetschius

Christ worked by principle, and the Sabbath was for rest, only to be broken BY **WORKS OF MERCY AND NECESSITY.**

Voice 3: 1-6

Compassion Mark 3:5.

Mark 3:4 – to withhold help is next door to murder.

JESUS ASKED COOPERATION FROM THE ONE HEALED. Mark 3:29.

Twelve Apostles

Appointed Mark 3:13-19. He saw the leaders of strength.

He chose them so they could be more intimately HIS 3:13 to hear His message 3:14, and so they could be clothed by His power 3:15.

    A) Peter (surnamed

Simon), James and John (surnamed sons of Thunder) had **STRONGEST PERSONALITIES, MOST GIFTED.**

B) The reflective type, slower to speak or believe:

Andrew, Philip, Bartholemew and Thomas.

C) Practical men, given to details, businesslike: Matthew, James, the son of Alpheus, Thaddeus, Simon the Caananite and Judas.

Mark 2:1 – 12 A SINNER MEETS HIS SAVIOR sick of Palsy – "My son, THY SINS BE FORGIVEN THEE."

ONLY GOD CAN FORGIVE SINS.

Matthew joins the team - Mark 2:13 – 17.

Here are:

1) Gathering his forces – being first a preacher, moving into the danger zone

2) The First Miracle – his authority, already noted

3) Various Healings – 1:29-45.

A) He had contacted several men (the world) he had contacted demons, the underworld, now he contacts the Father, the upper world 1:35.

B) Strength must be gained before strength can be given.

C) Give to God the best hours of the day and He will help you in the worst hours.

Christ was not one to settle down. From the popularity and throngs of Capernaum he moved out to the smaller, strange places 1:38, for sin and need were there.   1:39.

For THE FIRST TIME MARK SHOWS THE ELEMENT OF FAITH ENTERING THE SCENE FOR MIRACLES 1:40.

4) A Sinner Meets His Savior – Sin Which is at the base of all other ills. Jesus saves.

5) Matthew joins The Team

2:13-17 Levi original name. publican – receiver of custom.

a) He was under suspicion for he was the agent of a government that collected taxes by encouraging graft and dishonesty. (Rome).

6) Facing Controversy 2:18-22

Opposition springs from Christ's apparent indifference to their ceremonies.

7) By the Seaside 3:7-12

Mark pictures demons bowing before the Deliverer. 3:11.

8) The Unpardonable Sin – giving Satan credit for work of the holy spirit. 3:28-30.

- Satan is too smart to undo his own work. Mark 3:23-26.

CHRIST COULD NOT DO THESE MIRACLES HAD HE NOT FIRST DEFEATED SATAN. THAT BLASPHEMY IS FINAL AND IRREMEDIAL CONFUSION IN MORAL VALUES

9) The Family vs. the Kingdom

MARK 3:35

10) Wondrous Words   4:1-34
– parables

During Jewish harshness to hide from their eyes the truth, which is rejected would make their damnation worse 4:21-25.

Our language would be poorer by far, Did we not know the priceless words. The parables, so brief, yet so sublime, That from His lips did fall.

> 4 miracles – show
>   power over nature

demons disease and death.

Nature 4:35 – 41. (peace be still)

Rebuked the wind

5:8 Come out of the man thou unclean spirit

WE ARE safer in a storm with Christ than in a calm without Him. Power over demons.

5:1-20.

Come out of the man thou unclean spirit—

--My name is Legion for we are many.

"Go home to thy friends and tell them how great things the Lord hath done for thee.************

Lack of faith may be as real a handicap as an actual opposition to the work of God

Demon possession suggests the desire of evil spirits for human habitation even as the holy spirit seeks our bodies for His abode.

Evil passions

Lawless and unrestrained

Sin means restlessness
And self destruction

A menace to society
Isolates us from help of the good and FRIENDSHIPS of the wicked.

Demons accept a bestial abode.

The witness of a convert is often more effective among old associates.

See Power over disease

Woman clutching

Story -- 12 years of suffering 5:25-34.

TODAY WE STILL LIKE NEW CONVERTS TO WITNESS TO THEIR FAITH BEFORE THEY LEAVE THE PLACE OF HELP.

Conclusion

Dream – 2-11-93

I had had a baby with Jeff Baker, my schoolgirl sweetheart. We weren't married. We were then at a theater affair and he had pictures of the baby's first day taken by my sister Linda. The baby was in an awful mood and I begged him to save money so we could go to a studio for pictures. He said okay. He had a larged etched glass bowl that I had given him – so large that it would barely fit in the chair beside him. We were thrilled about the baby and he had his family there holding the child.

Then, I was back at home at Mother's house on 17th Street. She was doing the dishes late into a dark night but seemed unconcerned. There were no lights on except over the sink. I was at the computer which was also a video screen and was on the phone with Joanie from church and watching a video sister Linda had recorded. It was about earth and the future and my legacy, a large piece of land with lots of gravestones crowding my own – or some remembrance of my life there. It seemed everyone wanted to be buried next to me. It had lots of other pictures of earth and one about the reality which was oozing beige foam which as we watched all the earth sunk into, unreality. But she said even though earth would pass away there would be a reality for all of us – we would have friends that we could go places with and do things with.

An obit dream – I dreamed I was 29 or 30 and had married Jeff and had four children. My obit said Kathy M. Tyrity, wife and mother. Children: Silk-Sommer, Skyla, Royce-Daniel, and Tip Jovan.

Friends, this is my offering at this time for presenting ongoing suggestions to read and think about. I sure hope you find many more issues to read of the Holy Ghost Messenger Magazine. Rev. Kathy Tyrity.

(END)

*****

Made in the USA
San Bernardino, CA
27 January 2015